PEACE

Gardens of the Heart

PEACE

ELIZABETH CLARE PROPHET

SUMMIT UNIVERSITY PRESS®

GARDINER, MONTANA

For information, contact Summit University Press,
63 Summit Way, Gardiner, MT 59030.
Tel: 1-800-245-5445 or 406-848-9500
Web site: www.SummitUniversityPress.com

Library of Congress Control Number: 2012949318
ISBN 978-1-60988-158-0
ISBN 978-1-60988-159-7 (eBook)

SUMMIT UNIVERSITY ☙ PRESS®
Summit University Press and ☙ are trademarks registered in the
U.S. Patent and Trademark Office and in other countries. All rights reserved.

Cover and interior design by James Bennett Design

Printed in the United States of America
17 16 15 14 13   5 4 3 2 1

CONTENTS

Approaching the Garden

As we move through life, the key to our safe passage is harmony and balance. The ups and downs we encounter can all be viewed objectively from the balance point in the center of our hearts.

Visualize an ordinary seesaw in a playground—a flat board resting on a central pivot point. As a child mounts on each end of the board, they create movement. But notice that the center of the seesaw is absolutely stationary. The children can be moving wildly, franti-

cally on the ends, and the center is always balanced and stable.

The heart is that point of equilibrium. We can learn to go to this point of balance in our hearts—this point of peace. But it is also the point of power. We resolve all matters by the quietness and the all-presence of the power of peace.

One way to increase oneness with peace is to not take offense. If we don't take offense, we don't have to fight back. We can say something very quieting and calming and simply not be engaged. We do not argue. We do not accuse. We do not have discord.

For when peace has gone, everything has gone and there is nothing left. Things fall apart when there is no peace. When there is discord, you cannot hold a relationship together, you cannot hold a family together, a nation together.

And only when you come to a point where once again, through the power of interior equilibrium, you have found your balance does the power of peace begin to flow and do you start again to build those wondrous castles in the air—castles of hope—which may well materialize into the blessings you seek because you have kept the peace.

CLIMBING
WISTERIA

Come with me

to the garden of the heart.

Raise the latch of your attention

and watch the great golden gate

swing inward.

See the peaceful, winding pathway,

the verdant, protective hedges,

the trellised roses of love,

and hear the tinkle of falling water.

Be enfolded

in the surrounding peace.

The first

order of business

is to make peace

with ourselves.

Harmony

is the other side of peace

and peace,

the other side of harmony.

All people upon the planet

have a responsibility

to maintain peace

within themselves.

We are interested

in harmony, in justice,

in kindness and in love.

These compose the

foundation of true peace.

There will never

be peace on earth

unless it begins

with the individual.

To find

perfect peace on earth

is truly the art

and the science

of those who love.

When we are loving,

we are creators of peace.

Peace is

the acceptance

of what is.

Peace is

a profound understanding

that is at rest,

at equilibrium,

at the point of balance

in the heart.

Peace is a quality

whereby life itself

remains in balance,

absorbs great agitation

and is able to center

the mind and being

at the great point

where all is still.

When we

cultivate gratitude,

we are naturally

more balanced and

at peace.

We tend to think

of peace as love

more than anything else,

but peace is

power in restraint.

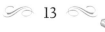

Let peace

be power within you.

Peace is the peace of water.

And the water of the mind,

the water of the desire,

the water of the memory,

the water in the earth body,

must be at peace...

Then you

can draw the power

from the water.

And when the

mighty wave does rise,

let it be tempered,

let it be disciplined.

We guard our heart

against intruders,

those inner and outer

pressures that disturb the

peaceful and harmonious

rhythms of love.

Remember

that all things

are yours to guard

and to treasure,

and you are the guardian

of your own

inner peace.

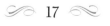

When peace is gone,

everything is gone

and there is nothing left.

Why is this?

Because things fall apart

when there is no peace—

relationships, families, nations.

Peace is not a

vibration of nothingness or

an absence of action.

Rather peace is a higher form

of the radiation of spirit

to be found, in part,

at the eye of a hurricane—

the peaceful calm of

the center of action.

When you have

a sense of peace,

you are at peace

about who you are

and what you are

and your wholeness.

Then and only then

do you have something

to offer anyone, any part of life.

When you have

the peace of wholeness,

you can attract from the

four corners of the heavens

more of that wholeness,

more of what you

are in reality.

There are times

when true peace

is best achieved

by willing involvement

in the battle of life.

Do not accept the false peace

where you desire

to be left alone.

A Robin's Egg

Give of your heart

and see how the

blossoms of peace

spring forth

in the hearts of others.

Every night

before you lay your

head upon your pillow,

make peace with those

you have hurt in any way.

And make peace with anyone

who has insulted, misrepresented

or harmed you.

Rather than

tossing and turning,

keep your soul

intact and at peace.

Turn your burdens

over to God and let go.

It's as simple as that!

Peace is not

a negative thing, not just

the absence of war.

Peace is a divine quality

evoked from the heart

of the Creator.

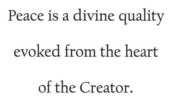

Peace must exist

not because men desire

the outer cessation

of hostilities, but because

men recognize

the realm of light within.

If we want to

create our worlds

and attract to ourselves

our dreams,

we must have peace.

Peace is happiness

in the twinkling of the eye

and the twinkling of the stars.

Rather than react

to another's anger or emotions

with more anger and emotions,

why not respond

out of the poise and centeredness

of the Tao

(the guiding principle

of all creation),

the place of peace.

Rather than

lamenting another's

shortcomings,

supply the difference

peacefully.

Surrender

the sense of struggle.

Sit back for a moment

and be at peace

and realize that nothing

is impossible to you.

The quality of peace

is often misunderstood.

People interpret

peace to be pacifism or passivity,

whereas the true nature of peace

is a dynamic

and active energy.

Inner peace is found

by changing yourself,

not the people who hurt you.

And you change yourself for yourself,

for the joy, serenity, peace of mind, un-

derstanding, compassion, laughter,

and bright future that you get.

When you release

all tension and dissatisfaction,

you will draw close to the

mighty inrush of peace.

We must be at peace

with ourselves,

with our innermost being,

with our neighbors,

with our friends,

with our loved ones and even

with our enemies.

The angels are

listening...

We need to

take the initiative

to make peace

with every part of life.

Take the quality of love,

or truth, or brotherhood, or oneness.

Meditate for a day on this quality;

think all day upon it.

You will be amazed

at the peace that will

intensify within you.

The world

is a chaotic place,

but let us keep our homes

as places of peace,

of joy and of happy families.

There is

no other receptacle

as important as the heart,

especially the hearts of

our children.

The heart is the receptacle

for balance, for peace

and for community.

We need to

have a peace,

an equanimity, a joy, a love and

a freedom that we communicate

to everyone, especially

to our children.

APPLE BLOSSOMS

In our hearts

dwells that cool

white flame of peace,

that soft flower radiance...

We see people

who are peaceful,

yet it is a passive peace.

It is not an active peace

which has the power,

centered in the very

heart and eye of peace,

to do battle with

the enemies of peace.

As water seeks its own level,

so angels gravitate to higher realms

and are able to assist you

in making contact

with your higher self.

The keys are love, harmony,

understanding and peace.

You can learn a lot

from other people

and the way they

appear to test you,

testing whether or not

you have gained the mastery

of your own world.

The mastery of your world

means that you can

create and maintain

your peace.

Contemplate

your own mortality

with peace in your heart.

You will see very quickly

how much more

you want to do in

your lifetime.

Is it not most desirable

to possess a peaceful response

to every problem of life,

to be that inner calmness

that faces life's tests

with tranquility,

to possess the poise

of victory?

It is well that each of us

draw a line in our lives

in observance of our integrity,

our self-esteem, our inner strength

and our inner peace—

and determine that no one

will cross that line

of our true identity.

Life in these times

is only as perilous

as is your absence

of true inner peace.

Let the quality of peace

be a power unto you.

Peace is as powerful

as the seven seas.

The law of rest

is the law of the relief,

even in music.

At regular intervals,

rest in absolute peace

within your heart.

Learn by the discipline of the mind

to go within—swiftly!

At the end of each day,

the heart needs an interval of rest.

It is a great moment

when we come to that place,

that point of stillness

and peace.

There is no peace

without honor.

There is no freedom

without love.

Will you accept, then,

the wind through

the olive tree of self?

Will you permit

the kiss of peace

to flood your souls?

It is difficult

for infinite peace

to occupy the spaces

within our beings

that can be filled

almost to the point

of saturation

with the disturbances

of outer conditions.

Men's hearts remain troubled

simply because we do not

become quiet for a moment

and permit the infinite peace

to seep through

the denser levels of

human thought and feeling.

If you would know

the joy of wholeness,

then freely, swiftly and peacefully

go about the process of eliminating

the unreal portions of the self.

As you overcome these difficult

and complex problems,

you become the person

who you really are.

Light from the window

of heaven will always blaze.

It will light the foam

and the whitecaps.

It will cool the mountain streams

and fevered brows. It will bring

peace to the hearts of men.

Peace

integrates you

with the fullness

of all that

you are.

The still small voice

beckons to us.

And that voice seeks to convey

peace to each individual,

peace in the valley,

peace in the city,

peace on the mountaintop,

peace in the heart

and peace in the soul.

Peace at any price

can betray,

whereas true peace

is an action

showering flowers of hope

to those upon the pathway.

When you contemplate

the vast ages past,

you will find that progress

was the order of the day only

during the ages of peace.

Never has a civilization moved forward

from an age of war, for destructive

activity can never produce

construction and progress.

You are linked

in the heart

with one another.

You must realize that

that which brings peace,

harmony, compassion and comfort—

all of that—is sustained by unity.

BELLS OF IRELAND

Do you hear

the rustling of the winds of peace

through the grass of humanity?

Do you hear

the hope for peace

springing full blown

from the hearts of men?

Do you hear

the calls for peace

from the hearts

of the babes

in their beds?

We must understand

that in the coming age

the way of peace

and enlightenment

is also a way

of action and strength.

Be warriors of peace.

Peace is a guardian action.

Peace takes care of life.

The power of peace

is an invincible power.

We have to be the warrior of peace

who stands fast against the forces

of anti-love, from within or without,

that try to separate us from

those we love.

When you are attuned

with the powers of creation,

the powers of creativity,

the powers of love and

the powers of light,

then you can hold

the pattern of peace.

Peace is a tremendous power,

the power of the seas,

the waters of the earth

and of the mountains.

Peace abides in every rock,

even within the

depths of the earth.

Peace is only skin deep

if we become offended

at little things and angry

when someone steps on our toes.

There is never any reason

in any situation

to take offense.

Recognize

that in the struggle

for integration and reality,

there are times

when even peace

becomes turbulent.

Determine to

maintain peace

no matter what is

happening around you.

Go within your heart

and be an observer

of the passing scene

rather than a cork

bobbing on the waves.

Do you

have troubling,

knotty situations in your life?

Don't hold on to your problems.

Always forgive others,

and let go of all that is not peace

in your life.

Practice patience and forgiveness

and tenderness and love.

Then no matter what is going on,

you will have inner peace.

If you would have peace

you must be peace

in the highest, dearest,

truest sense of the word.

Watch the streams

of light come down.

Watch the peace

that flows.

Watch the light

of your heart expand.

Watch the love

that glows.

Watch your consciousness

and your actions.

You can't get away from

the limitations of time and space

except through the heart.

And there

you can find peace.

Peace flows

as a gentle stream,

and were it to dash

as a mighty ocean,

it would still express

the perfection of

peaceful control.

The truth is that

we can comprehend

celestial radiance.

We can perceive the

pure and beautiful world

where the banner of

peace and love is unfurled.

Let

your heart

become

a pavilion of peace.

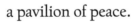

PAVILION OF PEACE

A MEDITATION

Will you take my hand

and come with me

into the world of dreams

where we shall create

an experience

of peace

in the

Pavilion of Peace.

There is created

by the angels

and the nature spirits

a pavilion of white alabaster

through which shines the light

never seen on land or sea,

the light of ten thousand

spiritual suns, the light

of the Eternal One.

Through the walls

of our alabaster

Pavilion of Peace

there gleams now this radiance.

There are four sides to our pavilion

and three magnificent domes

on each side—two below

and one above.

The gates of the pavilion

are open,

and six mighty seraphim

stand at each gate

to lead you upward

to the

Pavilion of Peace.

The mighty

organ of peace

is radiating out

that ethereal sound

which is soundless

but which rises

to crescendos

of peace.

And thus we see

the difference between

activity and greater activity.

For peace is not

an absence of action

but a higher form

of the radiance of God—

crystal glaciers all sparkling

as in a midnight sun.

A blue-white radiance

surrounds the Pavilion

and shines like a comet

in the sky of consciousness.

The vibration of peace

has the potential,

the vast and wondrous potential,

of increasing its own vibratory action.

And do you know

that there is a link

between happiness

and the increase

of the vibration

of peace?

Will you enter

with me now

the gates of the

Pavilion of Peace ?

Hear the sweet bells

ring out melodic joy that

peace can prevail.

Seven snow-white doves

are carrying a banner in their bills,

and they flutter at the gateway

as you enter.

The banner, in letters of gold,

billowing in a soft, gentle wind,

reads "Peace."

For there is

no other feeling

that can come

into the pavilion

save peace.

Now we see

the thirteenth dome—

an inner spire rising

and a beautiful brick mosaic

formed within it.

And there in gold,

stamped within a Maltese cross

of perfect balance,

is the word "Peace."

It is as though

the very

physical heart

wants momentarily

to pause and drink in

the scene of peace...

Seven rays are seen

coming down from the center

of the central dome,

white at the point of blending.

The gentlest of pastel hues

are to be seen upon the floor

where the reflected rays

gently position themselves

as though they were

seven votive flames.

Serenity,

bubbling as a gentle

fountain from the heart,

speaks of the quietude of peace.

This is a vital peace,

a peace surrounded

with feelings of light

and air and motion

and creativity.

You are offered

a gift this day:

a miniature replica

of the Pavilion of Peace

encapsulated within your heart.

This gift is given in memory

of your journey to

the Pavilion of Peace.

Remember this gift...

If you were to journey

to a far-off land

and meet a great ruler or king,

one who could give you

the greatest of gifts,

wouldn't you carry this gift

to the place where you dwell

and place it in a position of honor?

Would you not speak of it

to all whom you would meet,

especially those

who were wise enough

to understand it?

Likewise consider the

gift offered this day.

This gift can be

a point of contact for you

with universal peace.

It can, on the instant,

bring you into

the realms of peace.

If you accept this gift,

all you have to do

when all around you is turbulent

and you are in distress and in confusion

is to see the miniature

Pavilion of Peace

in your heart

and repeat as many times

as you like,

"I need thee,

O Peace.

Show forth thy light!"

And it shall be so...

SUMMIT UNIVERSITY ☙ PRESS®
Gardens of the Heart Series

Love	*Compassion*
Hope	*Gratitude*
Kindness	*Forgiveness*
Peace	*Joy*

SUMMIT UNIVERSITY ☙ PRESS ESPAÑOL™
Jardines del corazón

Amor	*Compasión*
Esperanza	*Gratitud*
Bondad	*Perdón*
Paz	*Alegría*

For other titles by
Elizabeth Clare Prophet,
please visit

www.SummitUniversityPress.com